Numbers in a Row

An Iowa Number Book

Written by Patricia A. Pierce and Illustrated by Dorothia Rohner

Special thanks to:
Antonia, Nico, Sophia, Ariana, Teo, Darnell, Mario, Monquia, Madeline, Colin, and Caitlin for posing as models. Iowa Historical Society, Bot Z Boo the Clown (Nancy), Caleb and Russ at University of South Dakota, University of Iowa Libraries, Bily Clock Museum, National Farm Toy Museum, Swedish Heritage and Cultural Museum, Tennessee Aquarium, and the National Mississippi River Museum and Aquarium for providing reference materials.

Ice Cream Capital of the World® and Blue Bunny® are used with permission from Wells' Dairy, Inc.

Sleeping Bear Press™

310 North Main Street, Suite 300
Chelsea, MI 48118
www.sleepingbearpress.com

© 2006 Thomson Gale, a part of the Thomson Corporation.

Thomson, Star Logo and Sleeping Bear Press are trademarks and Gale is a registered trademark used herein under license.

Printed and bound in China.

First Edition

10 9 8 7 6 5 4 3 2 1

Library of Congress Cataloging-in-Publication Data

Pierce, Patricia A., 1967-
Numbers in a row : an Iowa number book / written by Patricia A. Pierce;
illustrated by Dorothia Rohner.
p. cm.
Summary: "Iowa's history, inventors, industry, livestock, and more are introduced using rhymes and numbers. Detailed expository text provides in-depth state fact information"—Provided by publisher.
ISBN 1-58536-164-X
1. Iowa—Juvenile literature. 2. Counting—Juvenile literature. I. Rohner, Dorothia. II. Title.

F621.3.P55 2006
977.7—dc22   2006002351

With love to John, Andrew, and Jared
With prayerful hearts may we count our numerous blessings.

My gratitude to all my students; may your love of learning never cease.

My appreciation to Amy Lennex, Sleeping Bear Press, and Dorothia Rohner
for all their talent and hard work in making another wonderful book come to life.

PATRICIA

❀

For Gina, Hans, Lisa, Mena, Tana, Magda
and our childhood memories of Iowa spent picking black caps
on Indian Lookout with Grandma and Grandpa.

DOROTHIA

Creative ideas were jumping in the mind of a young boy from Blairstown as he watched circus tightrope walkers and trapeze artists taking flying leaps into safety nets, then bouncing up into incredible twists and crowd-pleasing somersaults. This gave George Nissen the inspiration for his invention, the trampoline.

Using material found at a junkyard, Nissen began tinkering with his idea. After several years of improving his "bouncing table," he then registered "trampoline" as a trademark for his invention.

Nissen, a gymnastics champion from the University of Iowa, used his skills to promote his invention by performing for crowds. A picture of Nissen jumping with a kangaroo was one of his best promotional ideas! His hard work and influence have made trampolining an Olympic and worldwide sport. Nissen proved that creative thinking can bounce into new inventions!

one
1

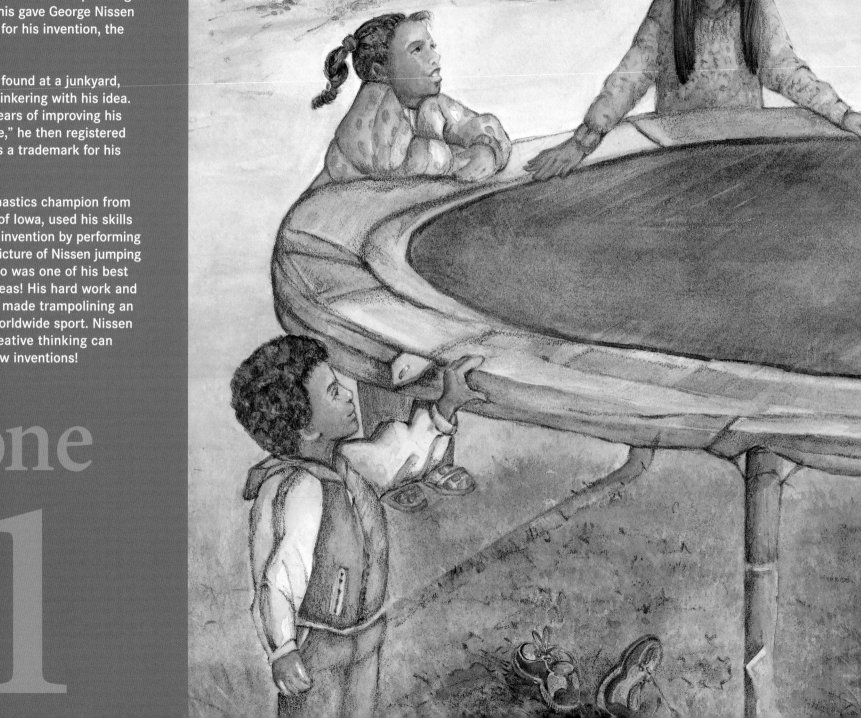

1 trampoline
with a mat firm and tight,
helps me jump and bounce
to an amazing height!

2 water towers,
can really perk you up.
One is a coffeepot,
the other is a cup!

Välkommen (welcome) to Stanton, where Swedish heritage pours from its water towers. In 1971 a decorative Swedish paint design, along with the addition of a spout and handle, changed an ordinary water tower into a giant-looking coffeepot. The water tower stands 125 feet high and holds 40,000 gallons. A second water tower, designed to look like a Swedish cup, was built in 2000. This tower is 96 feet tall and holds 150,000 gallons.

These unique towers are appropriate in Stanton, the hometown of Virginia Christine, the "Mrs. Olsen" in classic Folger's coffee commercials, and are popular tourist attractions along with the Swedish Heritage and Cultural Center. Stanton's heritage is also found in yearly traditions such as children in Swedish costumes performing traditional dances, and men serenading the public by singing *Beautiful May*.

two

2

"A band ought to have a sound all of its own. It ought to have a personality," claimed big-band leader Glenn Miller. Miller and his orchestra proved their unique sound and style of swing music, similar to jazz, and recorded 70 top ten hits between 1939 and 1942. Miller's music is celebrated annually in Clarinda, his birthplace, at the Glenn Miller Festival. Miller is also remembered for his patriotic devotion during World War II.

Mason City's musical talent, Meredith Willson, gave tribute to Iowa through his masterpiece, *The Music Man*. This musical, inspired by his hometown, premiered on Broadway in 1957. Music Man Square in Mason City honors Willson.

Another noted musical talent, Andy Williams, from Wall Lake, is well known for his stunning singing performance of "Moon River." He was also the star of *The Andy Williams Show*. These three musical talents showcase the sound and personality of Iowa!

three

3

Glenn Miller

Meredith Willson

Andy Williams

3 musical men
wrote songs we love to sing.
Dancing with a partner,
we waltz, sway, and swing.

Have you ever been to an orchard and noticed all the tall trees growing in orderly rows? If so, then it's easy to understand why in 1872 Jesse Hiatt would cut down a seedling that sprouted between the rows of his orchard in Madison County. When that resilient seedling, a cross between two different varieties of apple trees, continued to grow back, Hiatt then decided to let it grow.

For years he patiently tended to the tree before it produced fruit. He loved the aroma and texture of the crisp, crunchy, sweet, juicy apple. He named it "Hawkeye" in honor of Iowa and began promoting his discovery.

"My, that's delicious," agreed the president of Stark Bro's Nursery after tasting Hiatt's Hawkeye apple. The nursery bought the right to propagate it and renamed it "Delicious." Today, the Red Delicious apple is one of the most popular and widely grown apples in the United States.

four

4

4 Hawkeye apples,
so tasty and red.
Their Hawkeye name was changed
to Delicious instead!

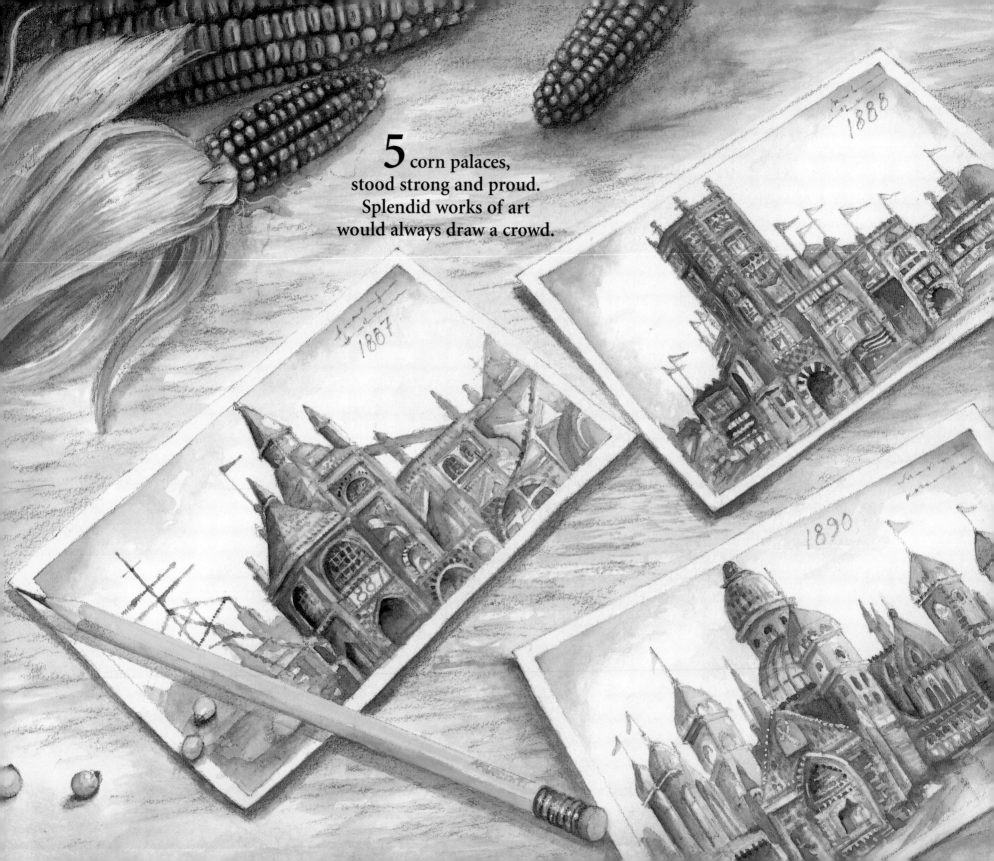

5 corn palaces,
stood strong and proud.
Splendid works of art
would always draw a crowd.

In Iowa corn is king and every king needs a palace! A corn palace was built from an abundant "king" crop in Sioux City in 1887. The palace was covered with corn and grain arranged in beautiful patterns and the inside was decorated with spectacular murals. Large crowds attended the first Corn Palace Festival and enjoyed parades, dances, fireworks, and concerts.

From 1888 to 1891 the corn palaces and festivals were even more impressive than the previous year. The palaces continued to be marvels of beauty. The fifth palace was so large that a special archway had to be built to allow traffic to pass through. Cold drizzly weather however, kept attendance low and finances became a problem.

The golden corn palace days ended after the Great Floyd River Flood devastated Sioux City in 1892. However, Iowa continues to lead the nation in corn production and its king crop rules in the numerous ways it is used.

five

5

What treat would you choose—chocolate or ice cream? It is believed that a young boy's struggle to make this decision was the inspiration behind the invention of the Eskimo Pie!

Christian Nelson, a teacher from Onawa, owned a candy shop and discovered a way to allow the boy to have both treats. He experimented with many different ways to make chocolate stick on ice cream. Finally, he discovered cocoa butter was the perfect adhesive.

Nelson called his creation "I-Scream-Bar." He teamed up with chocolate maker Russell Stover, and it was decided to change the name to "Eskimo Pie." In the early 1920s Eskimo Pies were often selling at the rate of one million daily!

You can treat yourself to an Eskimo Pie today, but you may have to chose between an Eskimo Pie with dark chocolate coating, milk chocolate coating, strawberry flavored swirl with a cake crunch coating, or the no-sugar-added ice cream bar.

six

6

6 Eskimo Pies—
ice cream on a stick.
"I scream" for ice cream.
Quick! Give me a lick!

Snake Alley in Burlington is listed in *Ripley's Believe It or Not* as "the crooked-est street in the world." It consists of five half-curves and two quarter-curves and climbs 58.3 feet over a distance of 275 feet. That's like going up approximately the height of a six-story building over about the distance of a football field!

Limestone curbing and blueclay bricks were used in the construction of Snake Alley. It was constructed in 1894 to create a shortcut to the downtown business district and was thought to be used as a testing route for horse-drawn fire trucks. Legend states that if a horse could take the curves at a gallop and still be breathing when it reached the top, it was judged fit for the fire department.

Today instead of horses, cyclists compete on Snake Alley as part of a physically challenging bicycle race course. The Snake Alley Art Fair also brings thousands of visitors to this historic landmark each year.

seven
7

7 fast cyclists,
bike up a curvy street.
Racing on Snake Alley
is a difficult feat.

Look at that snout! Not a pig's snout, but the snout of a paddlefish found in the Mississippi River. With its large mouth and a long, paddle-shaped snout, paddlefish are easy to distinguish from other fish. Paddlefish can grow to seven feet long and have a gray, shark-like body. They are also known as "fresh-water whales" because they filter feed as whales do, opening their mouths wide and using their gills to filter plankton.

These unique fish can be seen swimming at the port of Dubuque in the National Mississippi River Museum and Aquarium. Historically, Dubuque was an important center of fur trading and lead mining. Dubuque was the first city founded in Iowa and named after the French fur trader Julien Dubuque. He befriended the Native Americans in the area and was granted rights to mine their land for lead.

eight
8

8 paddlefish,
swimming in a tank,
at the port of Dubuque,
on the Mississippi bank.

9 circus clowns,
with a pig as a friend.
Can you find the clown
with the big rear end?

Ladies and gentlemen and children of all ages would laugh in delight as Frank "Felix" Adler waddled in his clown suit with padded hips and rear end! Funny Felix, the "King of Clowns," grew up in Clinton and performed for the Ringling Brothers and Barnum and Bailey Circus.

A pig was part of Felix's act. He trained pigs to climb a ladder and slide down a greased slide. The pigs were rewarded with milk from a baby bottle.

Felix often performed in Clinton and donated the proceeds of the programs to the YMCA. The Felix Adler Discovery Center in Clinton honors his memory and each June the town celebrates "Felix Adler Days."

The town of McGregor, home of the Ringling brothers for 12 years, also shines under the Big Top spotlight. Before becoming "The Greatest Show on Earth," the young brothers used a goat and dogs as their "wild animals" in their performances under a clothesline tent!

nine
9

10 grunting pigs,
trying to stay cool
like to roll around
in their muddy pool.

Iowa ranks first in hog production. There are approximately five pigs for every one person in Iowa! The pork industry creates more than 63,000 jobs for Iowans.

The history of Iowa's pigs can be seen firsthand at the 1850 pioneer farm site at the Living History Farms in Urbandale. Here you can see the Ossabaw (pronounced aw-saw-baw) Island pigs, similar to the pigs that would have been around in 1850. Farmers at that time needed a pig that could take care of itself. These pigs of the past had longer snouts to dig for their food, such as acorns and roots. The pigs were also fed corn, scraps, and slop.

Today's pigs live in a climate-controlled building where large fans and misters keep the pigs cool during the summer. Pigs are unable to sweat, so the 1850's pigs rolled in mud to stay cool. The mud also protected them from getting sunburned. In the winter the longer hair and the higher amount of body fat of the Ossabaw pigs kept them warm.

ten
10

11 spine-leafed yucca,
a beautiful sight to see.
Visit the bluffs of Loess Hills
and I think you will agree.

The Loess Hills (pronounced "luss") rise unexpectedly to heights of 200 feet for nearly 200 miles along Iowa's western border. This unique landform holds more prairie tracts than anywhere else in Iowa. The spine-leafed yucca that blooms in this geological wonder is one of the unusual plants that thrive in the Loess Hills Nature Preserve in Monona County. Rare animals found in the Loess Hills include the grasshopper mouse, prairie rattlesnake, and yucca moth.

Loess is a buff to yellowish brown, wind-deposited soil, composed mainly of silt left from glacier activity during the ice age. The Loess Hills were created layer by layer over thousands of years! Only in China can you find loess deposits as deep and extensive.

When first deposited, the loess was smooth like a snow drift. Today the Loess Hills are rough and jagged due to erosion, and are extremely fragile. Strategies to prevent erosion are being carried out to preserve this irreplaceable landscape and its native species.

eleven
11

Dribble—dribble—pass—dribble—dribble—shoot—score! A sold-out crowd cheers as a basketball team of six girls take over the lead. Six girls? Shouldn't only five girls be on the court? No, not if you were watching a part of Iowa girls' athletic history.

Six-on-six style of play existed for 95 years from 1898 to 1993. Three players played offense while three other team-mates played defense on the opponent's offensive end of the court. The uniqueness of the game included the rules that neither the defense or offense players on the same team could cross the half-court line. Players were also only allowed two dribbles.

The six-on-six girls' basketball state tournaments were immensely popular, but after the passage of Title IX, Education Amendments of 1972, a desire came about to convert to the five-on-five style of play. In 1993 the Iowa Girls High School Athletic Union voted to end six-on-six basketball, but the love and excitement of the sport remains.

twelve
12

12 basketball players,
once played on the court.
The rules have changed,
but not the love of the sport.

The race is on! Sprint cars zoom around the half-mile oval track in Knoxville. The Knoxville Raceway is considered to be one of the most competitive and prestigious sprint car racetracks. The track surface is black dirt and provides fast, side-by-side competition.

The shape of the one-man sprint car looks basically the same as the first sprint cars used in the early days of racing. The small body of the car covers the engine and gas tank and the wheels are exposed without fenders. Modern day cars also have large wings mounted on the roll cage. The wings give the car better stability and are an added safety feature.

Located off the second turn of the raceway is the National Sprint Car Hall of Fame and Museum. Visitors can view more than 25 restored sprint cars and one of the largest collections of racing photographs, uniforms, trophies, and other racing memorabilia. This popular attraction deserves the winning checkered flag for its showcase of sprint car racing history.

twenty

20

20 sprint cars,
with wings on their tops,
zoom side-by-side
'til the checkered flag drops.

30 yellow soybeans
roll out of my hand.
Farmers grow this crop
in our rich fertile land.

Soybeans, a valuable Iowa crop, are part of our everyday lives. Each day we eat or use something made from soybeans! In fact, soybeans are often called the miracle crop.

The highly nutritional soybean meal is used for livestock feed. Iowa's pork, beef, poultry, and soybean industries work hand-in-hand to provide us with protein-rich foods. Soybeans contain all nine essential amino acids that are the "building blocks" of the body and are a necessary part of a healthy diet.

Soy products also help our environment. Soy ink makes it easier to recycle newspapers, and soy plastics biodegrade very quickly. A renewable fuel called soy biodiesel is also environmentally friendly.

Soybeans are not found only in fields and feedlots, but also play an important part in food products, candles, cleaners, crayons, hair care products, and truck bed liners! It is a miracle crop.

Travel back in time by visiting a unique museum in Spillville. The Bily (pronounced Beelee) Clocks Museum displays the beautiful, hand carved clocks of Joseph and Frank Bily. The brothers were farmers and carpenters. In their spare time they worked as partners on their wood carving projects.

Almost all their clocks have moveable mechanical figures and musical chimes. The brothers received, but did not accept any of the many offers for their elaborately detailed clocks. It is believed that in 1928 Henry Ford offered a million dollars for the "American Pioneer History" clock, but the brothers declined.

The Bily Clocks Museum also contains memorabilia from the world-famous composer Antonin Dvorak (pronounced Dvor-zhack). The Bily brothers acquired the building in which Dvorak resided in Spillville during the summer of 1893. The brothers donated, upon their death to the city of Spillville, the building and their clock collection, with the agreement that the clocks would never be sold or moved.

forty
40

40 Bily clocks
tick away the time.
Listen very carefully;
do you hear them chime?

50 scoops of ice cream,
   such a wonderful treat!
Help me to decide
   which flavor I should eat.

"One scoop of vanilla, please!" These words are often heard in Le Mars, "The Ice Cream Capital of the World®." Le Mars was given this title in 1994 because Wells' Dairy produces more ice cream in one location than any other manufacturer in the world.

Founded by Fred H. Wells in 1913, the Wells' Dairy is the largest family owned and managed dairy processor in the United States. The name BLUE BUNNY® was inspired by blue bunnies in a department store window at Easter time.

To produce their delicious ice cream, 75,000 cows a day are needed to supply the necessary amount of milk. Can you imagine 47 football fields covered in one-inch thick chocolate? That's how much chocolate coating is needed yearly for the ice cream bars! You could also make one million strawberry pies with the amount of strawberries purchased yearly. "Yum—on second thought—one scoop of vanilla, covered with chocolate and topped with strawberries, please!"

fifty
50

Students in Spirit Lake Community School District are learning firsthand the benefits of wind power. It is among the first school districts in the United States to use wind power as a primary energy source. The turbines not only provide power, but excess electricity is sold back to the local utility.

Farming the wind has been a growing industry for Iowa since a law was passed in 1983 requiring utilities to invest in wind power. Iowa wind farms continue to be a growing energy source.

Wind farms are clusters of wind turbines, each about as tall as a 20-story building, which can generate energy for thousands of households. Electricity produced from wind is clean, renewable, and helps protect our environment.

sixty
60

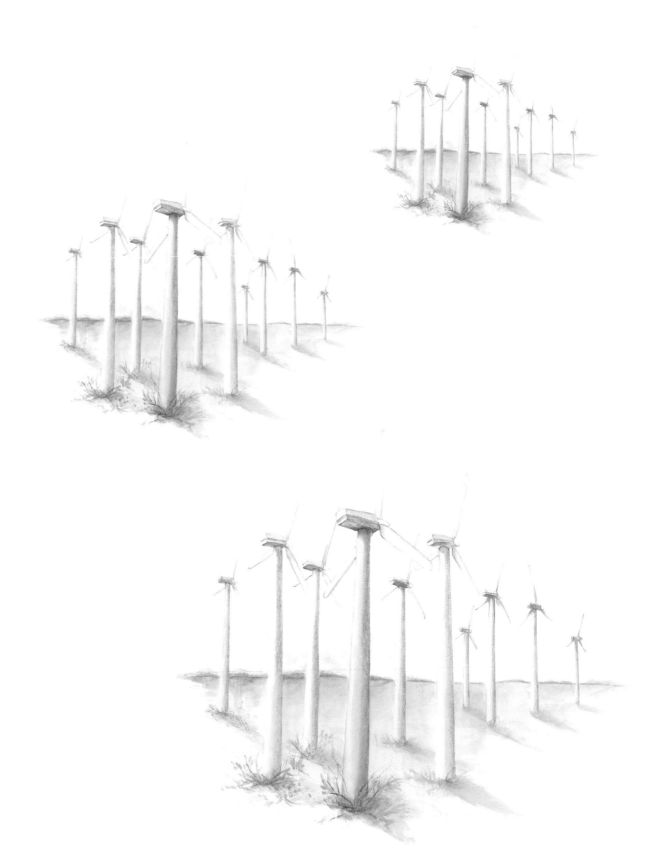

60 wind turbines
making energy.
Count the whirling blades.
One, two, three!

70 bright tulips
bloom in the month of May.
Slip on your wooden shoes
and march in the parade.

The clip-clop of wooden shoes, beds of colorful tulips, windmills, Dutch folk songs, and dances are part of the tulip festivals held each spring in Pella and Orange City to celebrate their Dutch heritage. Rev. Dominie Scholte led a group of Hollanders to America, and in 1847 they established a town named Pella, "City of Refuge." In 1870 Orange City was established by residents from Pella and named in honor of the Prince of Orange in Holland.

In honor of a tradition that demands that the streets be immaculately clean before the Queen and her court pass through, residents scrub the streets before the tulip festival parades. This popular ceremonial presentation, with street scrubbers wearing authentic costumes, is symbolic of the strong Dutch heritage of Pella and Orange City. The memory of the homeland of early Dutch settlers is kept alive by the brightly colored tulips and the sound of wooden shoes marching down the streets.

seventy
70

With tractors scaled down to $\frac{1}{64}$, $\frac{1}{32}$, or $\frac{1}{16}$ of their size, even a baby would appear to be a giant on a toy model farm. Opened in 1986, the National Farm Toy Museum in Dyersville contains over 30,000 farm toys and collectibles. The largest exhibit at the museum shows how tractors are scaled down in size from the real machine, and another interesting display shows how a farm toy is produced.

The idea for the museum started with the increasing growth of the National Farm Toy Show held annually in November since 1978. Known as the "granddaddy of 'em all," the show was started by Claire and Cathy Scheibe, publishers of *Toy Farmer* magazine. Collectors and dealers from across the country and world showcase their model toys and farms. Thousands of visitors view the realistic and impressive displays. Many intense hours of work are put into the displays, and attention is paid to the tiniest details.

eighty
80

80 farm toys
lined up in a row,
tractors, wagons, plows, and trucks,
all ready to go.

90 hot air balloons,
up, up, and away,
Come with me for a ride.
Hurry, don't delay!

What a view! It doesn't matter if the view is from the air or on the ground at the National Balloon Classic held each year in Indianola; the sight of colorful hot air balloons is spectacular. This hot air balloon competition attracts balloonists from all over the country to this nine-day ballooning event.

To win the competition, balloonists fly courses and earn points by dropping sand-filled bags on targets. Wind direction, time limits, and obstacles such as trees and power lines add to difficulty of the task.

The Nite Glo Extravaganza is also an impressive sight. The balloons, filled with air, are anchored, and the flames turned on to light up the balloons and create a marvelous night glow show. Balloons in special shapes also add to the excitement of the event.

Indianola is also home to the National Balloon Museum. Visit the National Balloon Classic and see Iowa from a different view!

ninety
90

What better place than Iowa to run 26.2 miles? Iowa offers several marathons, each one fun, friendly, fast, and (mostly) flat!

Does running 26.2 miles seem like a difficult task? Maybe not as difficult as organizing a marathon! In 1999 a Mason City Newman School student took on the challenge of organizing a running event, On The Road For Education, as an Eagle Scout project. It was a success and the start of a marathon tradition in Mason City.

The challenge of additional marathons can be found throughout the state. Iowa's golden dome is a welcoming sight in the Des Moines Marathon and the University of Okoboji Marathon provides a scenic course through their mythical campus. How about running in the Marathon-to-Marathon? The event begins in Storm Lake and ends in the town of Marathon!

one hundred 100

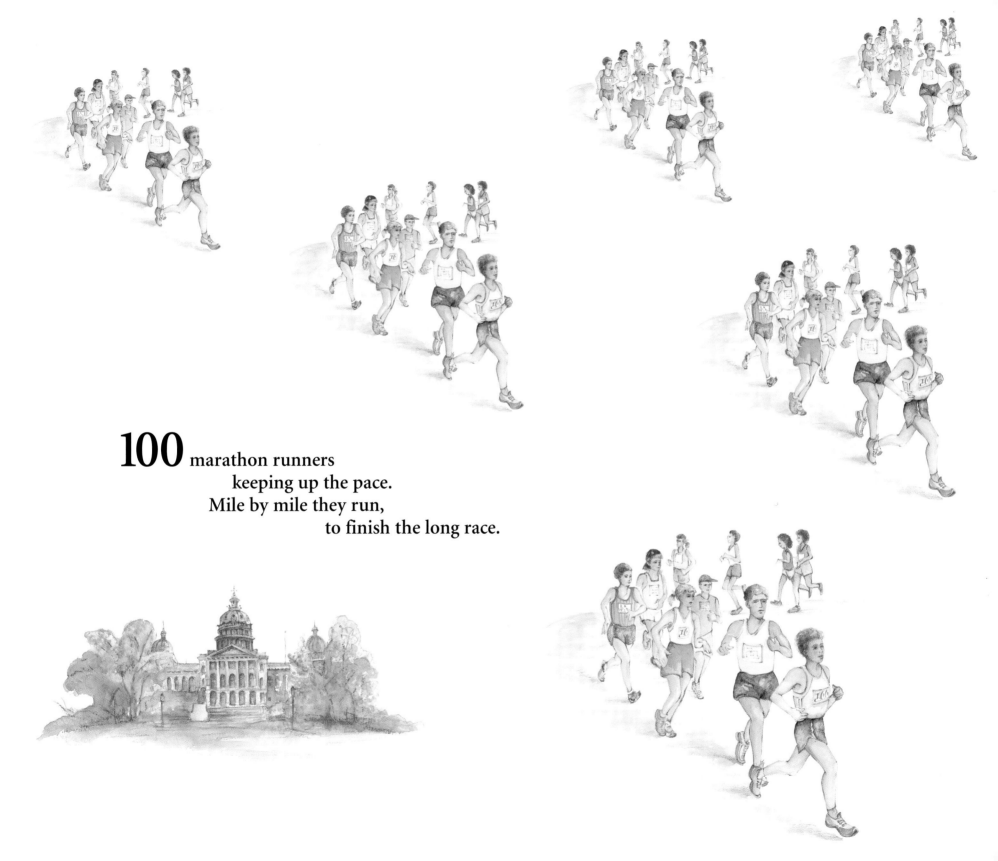

100 marathon runners
keeping up the pace.
Mile by mile they run,
to finish the long race.

Patricia A. Pierce

Author of *H is for Hawkeye: An Iowa Alphabet*, educator Patricia A. Pierce, M. Ed., and West Bend native, continues to share her love of writing and learning.

With fond memories of her high school athletic days, she was able to share part of Iowa girls' six-on-six basketball history while expressing her appreciation of her home state in *Numbers in a Row: An Iowa Number Book*. As a graduate of Loras College, Dubuque also holds a special place in Patricia's heart.

Patricia enjoys an active lifestyle, and along with writing, running is an outlet for her. She also treasures time spent with her husband John and sons Andrew and Jared. Learn more about Patricia at www.patriciapierce.com.

Dorothia Rohner

Dorothia Rohner is known for her botanical and nature paintings. For the past 17 years she has lived in the woodlands and bluff regions of Iowa and Nebraska. She earned her degree in biological pre-medical illustration from Iowa State University. Her illustrations have appeared in garden, science, and children's publications. *Numbers in a Row: An Iowa Number Book* is her second picture book. Her first picture book, *Effie's Image*, won *Learning Magazine's* 2006 Teachers Choice Award.

More of her work can be viewed online at www.paintedwings.com. She has two grown sons, Caleb and Winston, and lives with her husband Homer in rural Iowa.